*"In all humility but in perfect truth I claim
that if we attain our end through nonviolent means,
India will have delivered a message for the world."*
—MAHATMA MOHANDAS GANDHI,
ON THE EVE OF THE COMPLETION OF THE SALT MARCH

A TASTE OF FREEDOM

Gandhi and the Great Salt March

· · · · · · · · · · · · · · · ·

Elizabeth Cody Kimmel

ILLUSTRATED BY
Giuliano Ferri

WALKER BOOKS FOR YOUNG READERS
AN IMPRINT OF BLOOMSBURY
NEW YORK   LONDON   NEW DELHI   SYDNEY

If you saw him even once, you would remember him for as many years as you are blessed to live. I am a great-grandfather, but once I was young and strong with legs like little saplings. My sight is growing dim, but I can still see the face of Gandhi-ji, the Mahatma, as clear as a full moon on a cool summer night.

In those days our village was small and quiet. On that afternoon I tend to my chores as I do every day, but the goats and chickens run about nervously. My father and uncles discuss things in whispers. They are secrets not for my small ears. I want to know about the secret too. I do not have long to wait.

They begin to arrive in the afternoon, men and women from other villages. Why are they coming to Aslali? I did not know there were so many people in the whole world. They gather along the road to our village, the saris of the women making rainbows in the clouds of dust.

I ask my older brothers why all these people have come to our village. It is not a festival day. We do not have anything for them to buy. My brothers laugh at me and tell me I am too young, but the oldest, Rajiv, pulls me aside.

"The Mahatma is coming," my brother whispers.

The Mahatma! The Great Soul! His name is Gandhi. My father thinks that I am too young to listen to the talk of Mahatma Gandhi and his satyagrahis—those followers he calls his soul force. But I do listen. I know that Mahatma Gandhi has pledged to make our Mother India free from the rule of the British Raj. And he has promised that we will do so without hitting or hurting the British soldiers. The soldiers have guns and cannons. I do not know how the Mahatma believes we can beat them without fighting.

But I want to find out.

It is easy to slip away. There are so many people on the road and up trees and on rooftops. I climb a tree and inch out across the longest branch. My heart is beating so quickly I can hardly catch my breath.

I see a cloud of dust first. It rolls down the road, large and angry like a wild animal. A small man becomes visible through the dust. He is very old like my grandfather, but he walks so fast I wonder if he is flying. I do not need my brothers or my father to tell me who the man is. He is Gandhi, the Mahatma. The Great Soul has come to Aslali.

More faces appear through the dust. The Mahatma's satyagrahis are following behind him. There are ten, twenty, thirty, more than a hundred now, keeping step with him. The villagers cheer and throw flowers at Gandhi's feet. They bow their heads and press prayer hands to their foreheads as he passes. They sing and beat drums. "Gandhi-ji!" they call to him. "Gandhi-ji!"

He comes directly toward my tree. The branch I hold on to hangs low over the road. The Mahatma is almost close enough to touch! I squeeze my legs tightly around the branch and press my palms together. I try to close my eyes. But I peek.

Mahatma Gandhi is passing. He gazes up into my face. He wears small round spectacles. His brown eyes are merry. Under his little mustache, his mouth curls into a smile. Then he is gone.

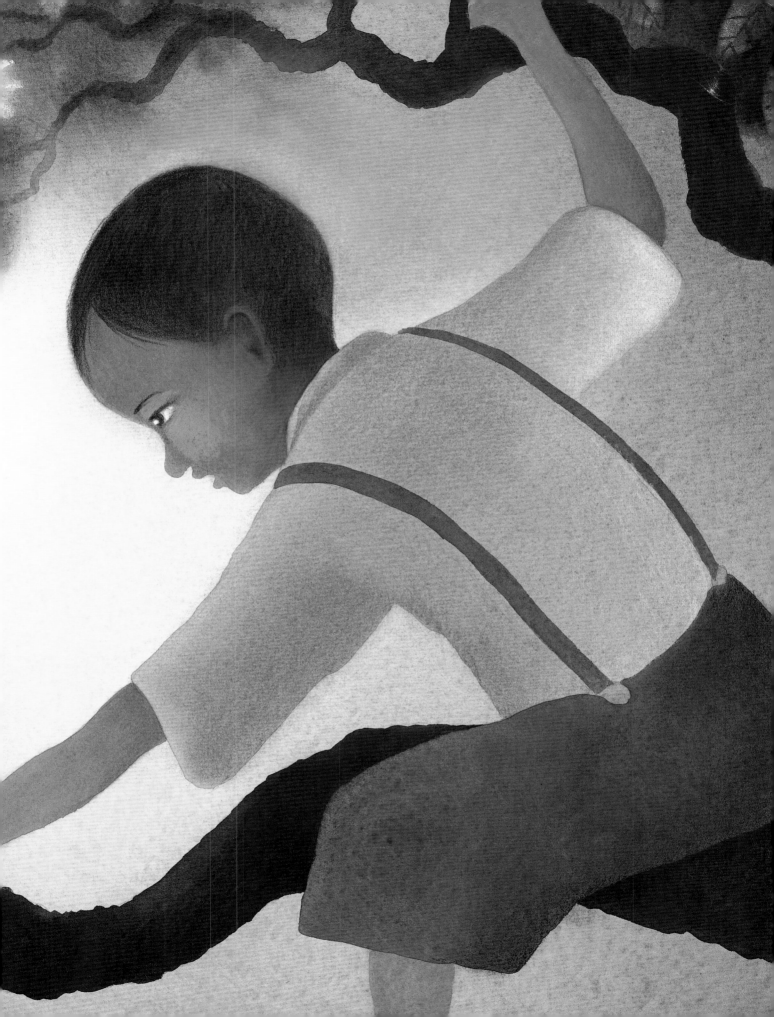

I do not go back home to my chores. I follow the crowd to the village center. I want to go where Mahatma Gandhi has gone. I wait, standing until my feet are very sore. But then the crowd begins to cheer. Mahatma Gandhi is speaking to us.

He is speaking to us of salt.

I cannot hear all the words that the Mahatma says. But I hear enough to understand. Gandhi is explaining that the way we will fight the British without hurting them is by using salt.

By using salt?

Before the Raj came, we gathered our own salt in India, which we could make from the earth near the oceans. Now my mother must buy her salt from the British. We are lucky we have a little money to spare for it. "We should not be made to buy salt or be forbidden to take what our Mother India freely gives us in her soil," my father grumbles. But how can we use salt to change the laws?

I hear rumblings in the crowd. They are angry at the Raj; they are tired of the unfair laws. They want freedom for India. They want to fight.

The Mahatma says we are all welcome to join him. He is going to march to the sea many miles to the south with his satyagrahis. When he arrives, he is going to make salt right there on the beach, even though British law forbids it. We may all make salt with him. The only thing we may not do is hurt or kill another person. Mahatma Gandhi wants to fight the Raj too, but he will do it only with peaceful actions.

I want to go to the sea with Mahatma Gandhi.

My brother Rajiv catches me packing a little bag late at night, when I am supposed to be asleep. I raise my chin and put my hands on my hips as my father sometimes does. I tell Rajiv I am going to make salt with Mahatma Gandhi, and he cannot stop me.

Rajiv is quiet for a time. Then he tells me he will come with me. "Our mother will rest easier knowing I am there caring for you," he explains. I say nothing, but inside I am very glad to know my brother will be at my side.

Gandhi and the satyagrahis are ready to leave by dawn. I join a long line of people as the Mahatma begins walking. His pace is very fast. Even Rajiv has to breathe heavily to keep up.

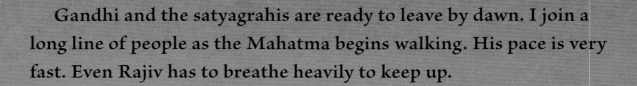

Each evening we approach a village and wave to the crowds that line both sides of the road. I see people on roofs and in trees. I wave at them too. Each night the Mahatma gathers all the villagers together and talks of peace. And of salt.

At dawn each day when we leave, many more join us. And though he looks thin and fragile, like a bird, Mahatma Gandhi always leads the way.

I have lost count of the days and nights when I begin to smell the scent of salt in the air. We are nearing the sea. Rajiv says that there are thousands of us now, following the Mahatma. The hum of many voices sounds like bees, blending with the crash of waves on sand. We have arrived in Dandi.

I have never seen the sea. It looks powerful and cool and delicious. The Mahatma walks straight toward the water. I am surprised that a wave rushes so fearlessly toward him. When he reaches the water, the wave dashes away. Mahatma Gandhi bends to the ground and picks up a lump of sea salt from the muddy sand. He holds it high in the air, and I feel a thrill rush through the crowd. I feel it race through my heart. Gandhi has broken the British law.

Up and down the beach, Indian men, women, and children are picking up lumps of sea salt. Rajiv says that all along the coastline, Indians are boiling the lumps down, making their own salt. I reach into the mud too. I come away with a pebble of sea salt held tight in my fingers. It looks wet and slick. I put out my tongue and touch the very tip of it to the salt.

Hundreds of thousands of Indians across the country joined
Gandhi-ji that day, taking back what Mother India gave us.
The British were very angry. They sent soldiers to the beach,
but the satyagrahis did not break their promise to Gandhi.
They did not try to hurt or kill the soldiers that came to arrest
them. Even our Mahatma himself was now imprisoned, but he
was not afraid.

I am a great-grandfather now. My sight is growing dim. Gandhi-ji has been gone for many decades. But I will never forget his face. I will never forget following the Mahatma to the beach of Dandi.

It is said that our Salt March shook the foundations of the mighty British Raj. It showed the strength of a people united in peace to fight for freedom. It is as real to me as if it happened this morning. Reaching into that muddy sand. Taking a pebble of salt, and touching it to my tongue.

No one ever forgets their first taste of freedom.

Gandhi spinning, late 1920s. Courtesy of Wikimedia Commons

AFTERWORD

· · · · · · · · · · · · ·

Thousands of Indians joined Gandhi on the Salt March, arriving on the beach at Dandi on April 5, 1930. The march took more than three weeks, and Gandhi and his followers walked over 240 miles. It would take many more years and tireless work and sacrifice before Gandhi would successfully lead his people to independence. But the Salt March saw the first and most important steps on this journey to India's freedom.

Gandhi remained in prison for more than eight months after the Salt March. In his absence, his followers staged a peaceful attempt to take over the British Salt Works at Dharasana. In keeping with Gandhi's teachings, they refused to defend themselves as they attempted to enter the factory. Countless numbers of satyagrahis were beaten to the ground by British soldiers. Even as they fell, the satyagrahis offered no resistance. Though the British retained control of the Salt Works, it was a moral victory for India. Many around the world were beginning to side with Gandhi and his peaceful ways.

On August 15, 1947, Gandhi's lifelong dream for his people came true with the official independence of India from British rule. A separate Muslim state, called Pakistan, was also established. Decades of work had finally paid off, but for Gandhi the victory was bittersweet. Tensions remained high between Hindus and Muslims. Some felt the Muslims had gotten too much; others thought they got too little. Hindus and Muslims fought each other. Horrified, Gandhi began a fast, refusing to eat at all. He said that he would fast to his death, unless and until the violence stopped. India's love for Gandhi was stronger than the white-hot rage that boiled between the Hindus and Muslims. The fighting stopped, but it was a fragile peace.

On January 30, 1948, in the early evening, Gandhi and several of his attendants made their way to a prayer meeting, as was his daily custom. A small crowd of people were gathered to watch him pass by. As Gandhi pressed the palms of his hands together in the traditional greeting, a Hindu man stepped forward and fired three bullets into Gandhi's chest. Gandhi uttered the name Rama, meaning God, before collapsing into silence. Minutes later, Gandhi was gone.

The most beloved man in India, and perhaps the greatest man of his time, was dead at seventy-eight. Only days earlier, Gandhi had told a visitor: "If I am to die by the bullet of a madman, I must do so smiling. There must be no anger within me. God must be in my heart and on my lips. . . . And if anything happens, you are not to shed a single tear." Gandhi's legacy lived on long after his assassination. His actions inspired people like Martin Luther King Jr. and Nelson Mandela to also seek change through nonviolent means. One small but determined man was able to bring a taste of freedom to so many people around the world.

FURTHER READING AND SURFING

BOOKS

Demi. *Gandhi*. New York: Margaret K. McElderry Books, 2001.

Ebine, Kazuki. *Gandhi: A Manga Biography*. New York: Penguin Books, 2011.

McGinty, Alice B., and Thomas Gonzalez. *Gandhi: A March to the Sea*. New York: Amazon Children's Publishing, 2013.

Pastan, Amy. *Gandhi: A Photographic Story of a Life*. New York: DK Publishing, 2006.

Wilkinson, Philip. *Gandhi: The Young Protester Who Founded a Nation*. Washington, DC: National Geographic Children's Books, 2005.

WEBSITES

The Gandhi Foundation: www.gandhifoundation.org

MKGandhi.org: www.mkgandhi.org/apinchofsalt/Chap01.htm

Pitara: www.pitara.com/magazine/people/online.asp?story=22

ROUTE OF DANDI MARCH IN INDIA

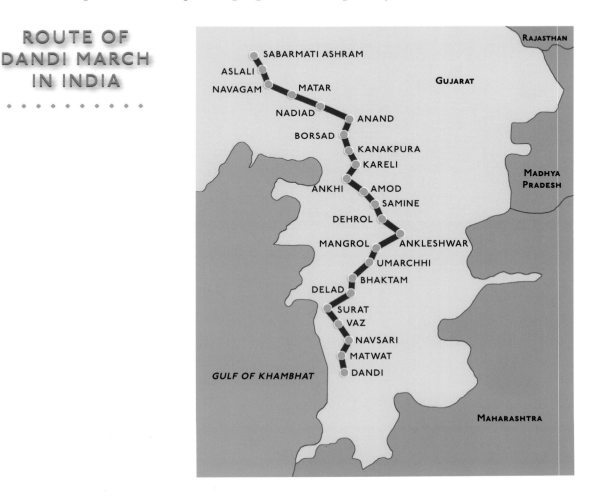

For Dr. Kathleen Nolan, who has taught me more than I ever imagined I could learn about peace, compassion, justice, and the importance of taking action to assist those in need. —E. C. K.

To Alice, Miriam, and Luca, because they can always enjoy the taste of freedom! —G. F.

Text copyright © 2014 by Elizabeth Cody Kimmel
Illustrations copyright © 2014 by Giuliano Ferri
All rights reserved. No part of this book may be reproduced or transmitted in any form
or by any means, electronic or mechanical, including photocopying, recording, or by any
information storage and retrieval system, without permission in writing from the publisher.

First published in the United States of America in February 2014
by Walker Books for Young Readers, an imprint of Bloomsbury Publishing, Inc.
www.bloomsbury.com

For information about permission to reproduce selections from this book, write to
Permissions, Walker BFYR, 1385 Broadway, New York, New York 10018
Bloomsbury books may be purchased for business or promotional use. For information on
bulk purchases please contact Macmillan Corporate and Premium Sales Department at
specialmarkets@macmillan.com

Library of Congress Cataloging-in-Publication Data
Kimmel, Elizabeth Cody.
A taste of freedom: Gandhi and the great salt march / Elizabeth Cody Kimmel; [illustrated by] Giuliano Ferri.
pages   cm
Summary: An old man in India recalls how, when he was a young boy, he got his first taste of freedom as he and his brother joined the great Mahatma
Gandhi on a march to the sea to make salt in defiance of British law.
ISBN 978-0-8027-9467-3 (hardcover) • ISBN 978-0-8027-9470-3 (reinforced)
1. Gandhi, Mahatma, 1869–1948—Juvenile fiction. 2. India—History—British occupation, 1765–1947—Juvenile fiction. [1. Gandhi, Mahatma, 1869–
1948—Fiction. 2. India—History—British occupation, 1765–1947—Fiction. 3. Civil disobedience—Fiction. 4. Nonviolence—Fiction.] I. Title.
PZ7.K56475Tas 2014   [E]—dc23   2013019877

Art created using watercolor and colored pencil
Typeset in Brioso Pro
Book design by Amanda Bartlett

Printed in China by C&C Offset Printing Co., Ltd., Shenzhen, Guangdong
1 3 5 7 9 10 8 6 4 2 (hardcover)
1 3 5 7 9 10 8 6 4 2 (reinforced)

All papers used by Bloomsbury Publishing, Inc., are natural, recyclable products
made from wood grown in well-managed forests. The manufacturing processes
conform to the environmental regulations of the country of origin.

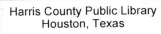